My Daily Affirmations

This Journal Belongs To

_____

Positive thinking helps with stress management and can improve your health. Practice overcoming negative self-talk and change your life for the better.

I WILL GROW POSITIVE THOUGHTS

Mood: ☹ ☹ 😐 ☺ 😃   Date:

I feel good about myself because...

Today, I forgive myself for...

Reflection

_____

_____

_____

_____

Reminder

_____

_____

_____

_____

DAILY SELF LOVE NOTE

I AM ENOUGH

Mood: ☹ ☹ ☺ ☺ ☺   Date:

I feel good about myself because...

Today, I forgive myself for...

Reflection

Reminder

_____   _____

_____   _____

_____   _____

_____   _____

DAILY SELF LOVE NOTE

I AM STRONG

Mood: ☹ ☹ 😐 🙂 😃   Date:

I feel good about myself because...

Today, I forgive myself for...

Reflection   Reminder

_____   _____

_____   _____

_____   _____

_____   _____

DAILY SELF LOVE NOTE

I AM IMPORTANT

Mood: ☹ ☹ 😐 🙂 😃   Date:

I feel good about myself because...

Today, I forgive myself for...

Reflection

Reminder

_____   _____

_____   _____

_____   _____

_____   _____

DAILY SELF LOVE NOTE

I AM EXTRODINARY

Mood: 😞 😦 😐 🙂 😃   Date:

I feel good about myself because...

Today, I forgive myself for...

Reflection

Reminder

_____   _____

_____   _____

_____   _____

_____   _____

DAILY SELF LOVE NOTE

I AM AN AMAZING HUMAN

Mood: 😦 😕 😐 🙂 😃   Date:

I feel good about myself because...

Today, I forgive myself for...

Reflection

_____

_____

_____

_____

Reminder

_____

_____

_____

_____

DAILY SELF LOVE NOTE

I AM A LEADER

Mood: 🙁 🙁 😐 🙂 😃   Date:

I feel good about myself because...

Today, I forgive myself for...

Reflection   Reminder

_____   _____

_____   _____

_____   _____

_____   _____

DAILY SELF LOVE NOTE

THERE IS NO ONE BETTER THAN YOU

Mood: ☹ ☹ 😐 ☺ 😃   Date:

I feel good about myself because...

Today, I forgive myself for...

Reflection

_____
_____
_____
_____

Reminder

_____
_____
_____
_____

DAILY SELF LOVE NOTE

I CHOOSE MY ATTITUDE

Mood: ☹ ☹ 😐 🙂 😄   Date:

I feel good about myself because...

Today, I forgive myself for...

Reflection   Reminder

_____   _____

_____   _____

_____   _____

_____   _____

DAILY SELF LOVE NOTE

I ALWAYS MATTER

Mood: ☹ ☹ 😐 ☺ 😃   Date:

I feel good about myself because...

Today, I forgive myself for...

Reflection   Reminder

_____   _____

_____   _____

_____   _____

_____   _____

DAILY SELF LOVE NOTE

I CAN GET THROUGH ANYTHING

Mood: ☹ ☹ 😐 ☺ 😃   Date:

I feel good about myself because...

Today, I forgive myself for...

Reflection

Reminder

_____   _____

_____   _____

_____   _____

_____   _____

DAILY SELF LOVE NOTE

I AM CAPABLE OF ANYTHING

Mood: ☹ ☹ 😐 ☺ 😄   Date:

I feel good about myself because...

Today, I forgive myself for...

Reflection   Reminder

_____   _____

_____   _____

_____   _____

_____   _____

DAILY SELF LOVE NOTE

I CONTROL MY OWN HAPPINESS

Mood: ☹ 🙁 😐 🙂 😃   Date:

I feel good about myself because...

Today, I forgive myself for...

Reflection

Reminder

_____   _____

_____   _____

_____   _____

_____   _____

DAILY SELF LOVE NOTE

I DON'T GIVE UP AND I WORK HARD

Mood: ☹ ☹ 😐 🙂 😄   Date:

I feel good about myself because...

Today, I forgive myself for...

Reflection

Reminder

_____   _____
_____   _____
_____   _____
_____   _____

DAILY SELF LOVE NOTE

I AM SPECIAL

Mood: ☹ ☹ 😐 🙂 😃   Date:

I feel good about myself because...

Today, I forgive myself for...

Reflection

_____
_____
_____
_____

Reminder

_____
_____
_____
_____

DAILY SELF LOVE NOTE

I LOVE ME

Mood: ☹ ☹ 😐 🙂 😃   Date:

I feel good about myself because...

Today, I forgive myself for...

Reflection   Reminder

_____   _____

_____   _____

_____   _____

_____   _____

DAILY SELF LOVE NOTE

I AM GRATEFUL FOR WHO I AM

Mood: ☹ ☹ 😐 ☺ 😄   Date:

I feel good about myself because...

Today. I forgive myself for...

Reflection   Reminder

_____   _____

_____   _____

_____   _____

_____   _____

DAILY SELF LOVE NOTE

I PUT MYSELF FIRST

Mood: ☹ ☹ 😐 ☺ 😃   Date:

I feel good about myself because...

Today, I forgive myself for...

Reflection

_____

_____

_____

_____

Reminder

_____

_____

_____

_____

DAILY SELF LOVE NOTE

I USE MY GIFTS WITH LOVE, GRATITUDE AND PRIDE

Mood: ☹ 😦 😐 🙂 😄   Date:

I feel good about myself because...

Today, I forgive myself for...

Reflection   Reminder

_____   _____

_____   _____

_____   _____

_____   _____

DAILY SELF LOVE NOTE

I AM NOT AFRAID TO FAIL

Mood: 🙁 ☹️ 😐 🙂 😃   Date:

I feel good about myself because...

Today, I forgive myself for...

Reflection

Reminder

_____   _____

_____   _____

_____   _____

_____   _____

DAILY SELF LOVE NOTE

I HAVE INNER PEACE

Mood: 😦 😕 😐 🙂 😃   Date:

I feel good about myself because...

Today, I forgive myself for...

Reflection

Reminder

_____   _____

_____   _____

_____   _____

_____   _____

DAILY SELF LOVE NOTE

I HAVE EVERYTHING I NEED WITHIN MYSELF

Mood: ☹ ☹ 😐 ☺ 😃   Date:

I feel good about myself because...

Today, I forgive myself for...

Reflection   Reminder

_____   _____

_____   _____

_____   _____

_____   _____

DAILY SELF LOVE NOTE

I TRUST MY INSTINCTS

Mood: ☹ ☹ 😐 ☺ 😄   Date:

I feel good about myself because...

Today, I forgive myself for...

Reflection

Reminder

_____   _____

_____   _____

_____   _____

_____   _____

DAILY SELF LOVE NOTE

I HAVE A KIND HEART

Mood: ☹ ☹ 😐 ☺ 😄   Date:

I feel good about myself because...

Today, I forgive myself for...

Reflection   Reminder

_____   _____

_____   _____

_____   _____

_____   _____

DAILY SELF LOVE NOTE

ALL MY WORDS HAVE POWER

Mood: ☹ ☹ 😐 ☺ 😃   Date:

I feel good about myself because...

Today, I forgive myself for...

Reflection

Reminder

DAILY SELF LOVE NOTE

I CAN BE ANYTHING I WANT TO BE

Mood: 😦 😞 😐 ☺ 😃   Date:

I feel good about myself because...

Today, I forgive myself for...

Reflection

Reminder

_____   _____

_____   _____

_____   _____

_____   _____

DAILY SELF LOVE NOTE

I HAVE RESPECT FOR OTHERS

Mood: ☹ 🙁 😐 🙂 😄   Date:

I feel good about myself because...

Today, I forgive myself for...

Reflection

Reminder

_____   _____

_____   _____

_____   _____

_____   _____

DAILY SELF LOVE NOTE

MY FAMILY IS PROUD OF ME

Mood: ☹ ☹ 😐 🙂 😃   Date:

I feel good about myself because...

Today, I forgive myself for...

Reflection	Reminder
_____	_____
_____	_____
_____	_____
_____	_____

DAILY SELF LOVE NOTE

I HAVE BIG DREAMS

Mood: ☹ ☹ 😐 🙂 😀   Date:

I feel good about myself because...

Today, I forgive myself for...

Reflection

Reminder

_____   _____

_____   _____

_____   _____

_____   _____

DAILY SELF LOVE NOTE

I AM PROUD OF WHO I AM

Mood: ☹ ☹ 😐 🙂 😀   Date:

I feel good about myself because...

Today, I forgive myself for...

Reflection	Reminder
_____	_____
_____	_____
_____	_____
_____	_____

DAILY SELF LOVE NOTE

I AM POSITIVE

Mood: ☹ ☹ 😐 🙂 😀   Date:

I feel good about myself because...

Today, I forgive myself for...

Reflection

Reminder

_____   _____

_____   _____

_____   _____

_____   _____

DAILY SELF LOVE NOTE

I WILL NOT COMPARE MYSELF TO OTHERS

Mood: ☹ ☹ 😐 ☺ 😄   Date:

I feel good about myself because...

Today, I forgive myself for...

Reflection

Reminder

_____   _____

_____   _____

_____   _____

_____   _____

DAILY SELF LOVE NOTE

I AM HAPPY FOR THE SUCCESS OF OTHERS

Mood: ☹ ☹ 😐 🙂 😄   Date:

I feel good about myself because...

Today, I forgive myself for...

Reflection

Reminder

_____   _____

_____   _____

_____   _____

_____   _____

DAILY SELF LOVE NOTE

I AM TRUSTWORTHY

Mood: ☹ ☹ 😐 ☺ 😃   Date:

I feel good about myself because...

Today, I forgive myself for...

Reflection

_____

_____

_____

_____

Reminder

_____

_____

_____

_____

DAILY SELF LOVE NOTE

I HAVE MANY GIFTS AND TALENTS

Mood: ☹ ☹ 😐 ☺ 😃   Date:

I feel good about myself because...

Today, I forgive myself for...

Reflection   Reminder

_____   _____

_____   _____

_____   _____

_____   _____

DAILY SELF LOVE NOTE

I CAN BE ANYTHING I WANT TO BE

Mood: ☹ ☹ ☺ ☺ ☺   Date:

I feel good about myself because...

Today, I forgive myself for...

Reflection

Reminder

_____   _____

_____   _____

_____   _____

_____   _____

DAILY SELF LOVE NOTE

I AM PATIENT

Mood: 😞 😟 😐 🙂 😃   Date:

I feel good about myself because...

Today, I forgive myself for...

Reflection   Reminder

_____   _____

_____   _____

_____   _____

_____   _____

DAILY SELF LOVE NOTE

I HAVE THE POWER TO MAKE MY DREAMS COME TRUE

Mood: ☹ ☹ 😐 ☺ 😄   Date:

I feel good about myself because...

Today, I forgive myself for...

Reflection   Reminder

_____   _____

_____   _____

_____   _____

_____   _____

DAILY SELF LOVE NOTE

I FIND WAYS TO SMILE OFTEN

Mood: ☹ ☹ 😐 ☺ 😃   Date:

I feel good about myself because...

Today, I forgive myself for...

Reflection   Reminder

_____   _____
_____   _____
_____   _____
_____   _____

DAILY SELF LOVE NOTE

I AM BOLD AND BEAUTIFUL

Mood: ☹ ☹ 😐 ☺ 😃   Date:

I feel good about myself because...

Today, I forgive myself for...

Reflection	Reminder
_____	_____
_____	_____
_____	_____
_____	_____

DAILY SELF LOVE NOTE

I HAVE A STRONG BODY AND MIND

Mood: ☹ ☹ 😐 🙂 😃   Date:

I feel good about myself because...

Today, I forgive myself for...

Reflection   Reminder

_____   _____

_____   _____

_____   _____

_____   _____

DAILY SELF LOVE NOTE

I LOVE LEARNING

Mood: ☹ ☹ ☺ ☺ ☺   Date:

I feel good about myself because...

Today, I forgive myself for...

Reflection

Reminder

_____   _____

_____   _____

_____   _____

_____   _____

DAILY SELF LOVE NOTE

I WILL NOT LET NEGATIVE THOUGHTS DICTATE MY LIFE

Mood: ☹ ☹ 😐 🙂 😃   Date:

I feel good about myself because...

Today, I forgive myself for...

Reflection

Reminder

_____   _____

_____   _____

_____   _____

_____   _____

DAILY SELF LOVE NOTE

I AM WISE

Mood: 🙁 ☹️ 😐 🙂 😀   Date:

I feel good about myself because...

Today, I forgive myself for...

Reflection   Reminder

_____   _____

_____   _____

_____   _____

_____   _____

DAILY SELF LOVE NOTE

I AM A PROBLEM SOLVER

Mood: ☹ ☹ 😐 🙂 😄   Date:

I feel good about myself because...

Today, I forgive myself for...

Reflection   Reminder

_____   _____

_____   _____

_____   _____

_____   _____

DAILY SELF LOVE NOTE

I AM FUNNY

Mood: ☹ ☹ 😐 ☺ 😃   Date:

I feel good about myself because...

Today, I forgive myself for...

Reflection

_____

_____

_____

_____

Reminder

_____

_____

_____

_____

DAILY SELF LOVE NOTE

I AM A GREAT FRIEND

Mood: ☹ ☹ 😐 ☺ 😃   Date:

I feel good about myself because...

Today, I forgive myself for...

Reflection	Reminder
_____	_____
_____	_____
_____	_____
_____	_____

DAILY SELF LOVE NOTE

I AM ADVENTUROUS

Mood: ☹ ☹ 😐 🙂 😄   Date:

I feel good about myself because...

Today, I forgive myself for...

Reflection   Reminder

_____   _____

_____   _____

_____   _____

_____   _____

DAILY SELF LOVE NOTE

I HAVE A PURPOSE IN THIS WORLD

Mood: ☹ ☹ 😐 ☺ 😃   Date:

I feel good about myself because...

Today, I forgive myself for...

Reflection

Reminder

_____   _____

_____   _____

_____   _____

_____   _____

DAILY SELF LOVE NOTE

NEVER FORGET YOU ARE ALWAYS ENOUGH. NEVER LET ANYONE CHANGE WHO YOU ARE!

I HOPE YOUR JOURNEY TO GROWING POSITIVE THOUGHTS CONTINUES.

Made in the USA
Monee, IL
13 December 2022